Personal Finance:

Guide to Saving Money, Budgeting, Paying off Debt and Improving Your Credit

By Susan Kilmer

Copyright © 2015 Provident Wellness

All Rights Reserved.

© **Copyright 2015 by Provident Wellness**

All rights reserved.

This document is geared towards providing exact and reliable information in regards to the topic and issue covered. The publication is sold with the idea that the publisher is not required to render accounting, officially permitted, or otherwise, qualified services. If advice is necessary, legal or professional, a practiced individual in the profession should be ordered.

- From a Declaration of Principles which was accepted and approved equally by a Committee of the American Bar Association and a Committee of Publishers and Associations.

In no way is it legal to reproduce, duplicate, or transmit any part of this document in either electronic means or in printed format. Recording of this publication is strictly prohibited and any storage of this document is not allowed unless with written permission from the publisher. All rights reserved.

The information provided herein is stated to be truthful and consistent, in that any liability, in terms of inattention or otherwise, by any usage or abuse of any policies, processes, or directions contained within is the solitary and utter responsibility of the recipient reader. Under no circumstances will any legal responsibility or blame be held against the publisher for any reparation, damages, or monetary loss due to the information herein, either directly or indirectly. Respective authors own all copyrights not held by the publisher.

The information herein is offered for informational purposes solely, and is universal as so. The presentation of the information is without contract or any type of guarantee assurance.

The trademarks that are used are without any consent, and the publication of the trademark is without permission or backing by the trademark owner. All trademarks and brands within this book are for clarifying purposes only and are the owned by the owners themselves, not affiliated with this document.

Introduction

I wanted to start off by thanking you for taking an interest in this book. The main purpose of **Personal Finance: Guide to Budgeting, Saving Money and Improving Your Credit** is to assist you in improving the way that you manage your finances.

More often than not when aspiring entrepreneurs fail at starting their business and growing their business, it is due to a lack in managing their business especially their finances properly. It is also correct to say that this lack of skillset is due to their bad personal financial habits.

Poor financial habits is not only an entrepreneurial problem but it is a basic household problem that is common among many people. This guide is designed to give you general recommendations on how to save money, how to budget, how to improve your credit and much more!

Enjoy!

Chapter 1

What is Budgeting and Why is it So Important?

Budgeting is the process of creating a system and process on how to spend and save your money. This system and process is called a **budget.** Creating a system allows you to determine in advance (if you stick with it) whether you will have enough money to do the things you need or want to do.

Budgeting also is the act of balancing your income with your debts and expenses. If your expenses outweigh the income coming in, then you have a major cash flow problem and you will end up sinking further and further into debt and will struggle getting out of it. If this is you, I'm glad you picked up this book.

Most people don't even realize they are spending more than what they are earning and are sinking into a financial hole they will have a hard time getting out of it.

Why is Budgeting So Important?

Since having a budget allows you to create a spending process for your money, if you stick with it, it will help ensure that you will hopefully always have enough money for the things that you need first, want second such as the things that you deem important to you.

Following a budget or spending plan will also help you get out of debt or at the very least help you get you into a process where you will eventually get out of debt.

Budget Projections, Planning and Forecasting

Once you create your initial budget and begin to use it, you will get a good feel for how it can help you keep your finances on track. Once you get used to this system, you will then want to map out your spending for the next 6 months to a year down the road.

By doing this, you can easily predict what your finances will be like and whether you will have extra money down the road. You can then identify ways to get out of the problematic time periods and keep your finances balanced and manageable.

Projecting your budget out into the future allows you also to forecast how much money you will be able to save for any personal goals such as buying a home, new vehicle or even going on vacation.

Creating a budget is typically created using a spreadsheet and it provides an organized and easy way of understanding of how much money you have coming in and how much money you are getting rid of. Creating this spreadsheet is an invaluable tool to help you prioritize your choices and your money no matter how much or little you may have financially.

Planning and monitoring your budget will also help you identify where your money is being wasted and how to make changes quickly before problems arise. When you start to see a breakdown of your income, expenses and spending habits you will be surprised what you find and how quickly spending will add up.

Simply put, a budget is an itemized summary of likely income and expenses for a given period. It helps you determine whether you can grab that bite to eat or should head home for a bowl of soup. It is typically created using a spreadsheet, and it provides a concrete, organized, and easily understood breakdown of how much money you have coming in and how much you are letting go. It's an invaluable tool to help you prioritize your spending and manage your money—no matter how much or how little you have. Creating a budget will help decrease your stress levels because with it, there are no surprises and you can make better financial decisions.

Chapter 2

Setting Up a Budget For the First Time

When you are setting up a budget for the first time, you ideally will want to have a place where you can record the money that is going in and out of your financial accounts and also a list of your expenses and your monthly payment due for each one.

Tools Needed:

- Spreadsheet Software **OR** notebook, pen and calculator (if no spreadsheet is available)
- List of Expenses, Bills and Debts
- Access to your current bank account statement (online or paper statements if applicable)

To set up your budget you will need make three (3) major columns either in the spreadsheet software or notebook you will be using. The three columns will have the following headings:

List of Expenses/Revenue, Day of the Month it is Due, Budget Month:

List of Expenses	Day Due	January	February
Rent	1st	$400	
Electricity	1st	100	
Water	1st	75	
Car Payment	15th	50	
Credit Card #1	23rd	25	
Total		$650	
List of Revenue	Day Due	January	February
Salary Paycheck #1	1st	$1000	
Salary Paycheck #2	15th	$1000	
Total		$2000	

| Net Profit/Net Loss | | $1,350 | |

You will want to make sure that when you are creating columns for the budget months, you will have enough columns for all 12 months for the year. Ideally, the minimum number of columns you will have is **14**, one for every month of the year, the day when the expenses or income occurs, and the list of income and expenses.

Under the different month columns you will want to put how much you will have to pay for those expenses. For credit cards and other debts that have a minimum monthly payment due, you want to put that amount. We'll explain why later.

For non-minimum payment debts that have costs that are variable such as utilities, you will want to put the most your bill payment has. The reasoning behind this is if you put the most you have ever paid in any given month, the assumption is that your payment will always be that same amount or less.

In the cells designated for column totals, you can manually total the amounts with a calculator or you can use the formula used to calculate a group of numbers. This is called the **SUM** formula.

The formula goes like this: =SUM(C2:C6). SUM means you want the spreadsheet to do an addition calculation. C2 and C6 can be exchanged for the first cell in that column with an expense # in it and C6 is the very last cell in that column.

For this example, I want to use the January Column so the formula will be =SUM(C2:C6), math wise it will be =SUM(all number starting from $400 through $25) which should end up **$650** in the example above.

Then you will want to do the same for the bottom half of those same columns, in the income section of your spreadsheet. You will want to put in what your typical salary will be or the income you have coming in, what dates and the lowest amount you typically get. You want to put the lowest amount you typically get because you want to plan for worst case scenarios.

As you get your income coming in, you can change those numbers to reflect the actual amounts but when projecting ahead of time, you want to plan for worst case scenario and put in the smallest amount you've ever had coming in and you wanted to use the same **SUM** formula using the cells where your income amounts are listed to calculate your total salary for that given month.

In the cells designated for the **Net Profit/Loss** amounts, you want to calculate how much you have left over after you pay your expenses. You can use the subtraction formula which is =X-Y where X is the cell that has the total income amount and you subtract Y which is the cell that has the total expenses amount in that column. In the aforementioned example it is =X-Y which translates into **=$1000 - $650**. When the formula totals it should be **$1,350**.

When you first create a budget spreadsheet, you can use the numbers in the aforementioned example until you get the hang of using formulas in the spreadsheet software. Then you can revise it with numbers in your specific situation.

Once you finish your spreadsheet, then you can look at it more in-depth and see how your monthly financial situation will end up. As you find out your exact bill payments due and your income amounts coming in, then you can change the assumed numbers to the actual numbers to get a more realistic view of your financial outlook.

Chapter 3

Budgeting Fundamentals

When creating your budget for the first time and really trying to account for the money coming in and out of your bank account, you will want to understand some basic fundamentals and key points:

Account for every single item you spend money on including discretionary items such as groceries, car fuel, gym memberships, salon appointments, new clothes. **TIP:** Think about everything you typically will want to spend on and include them into your spreadsheet.

When it comes to spending that isn't a debt or a bill, then put an amount in the spreadsheet that you want to set money aside for and treat it like a monthly payment or a bill. When budgeting for the first time you want to think about what your ideal situation will be and if you find that after calculating everything in your spreadsheet and you end up with negative amount of money left over, then you need to cut spending. In this case, you cut the discretionary ("wants") first.

You have to be realistic and honest with yourself. You want to list every bill and debt you have. Even if it's a payment you only make once a year, include the amount as a regular monthly payment. If the money set aside isn't spent on for that month because it's not due for 2 months, then it's okay because that money will just end up back in your bank account.

You also want to also start taking a hard look at your spending habits and also identifying ways where you can lower the amounts you spend on discretionary items such as car fuel, groceries, clothing, etc. which we will cover in the next chapter

Chapter 4

Cutting Costs

The next step in identifying various ways for you to cut your discretionary spending especially if you are adamant on maintaining your lifestyle. One way you can cut spending is to first start with your grocery spending.

If for example, you normally spend $500 on groceries per month then you can utilize websites that offer coupons so that you can still get the items you need for less. To get coupons you can get them from the manufacturer website, newspaper circulars, coupon websites and you also get coupons from the cashier at your normal grocery store when you check out.

A few years ago, couponing was a great way to get some items **FREE** or near free until television shows starting airing about thrifty individuals and as a result grocery store chains and product manufacturers stopped offering as many coupons for their products or no longer offered double or triple coupon opportunities so its somewhat harder but using coupons are still effective.

Keep in mind, grocery stores still have a 6 week cycle where they will change their product prices to their desired lowest amounts. You will need to time your coupons for these days.

For example, if cheese slices are let's say $3.99 for a 16 singles pack, and at their lowest they are $2.99, you will want to use your coupon then. The coupon may be for a dollar off. So instead of getting the cheese for $3.99 or $2.99 plus tax, with the coupon you will get it for $1.99. That is nearly 50% off. Keep in mind, the coupons typically offered enable you to get closer to 80% off.

There have been complaints at times where people have stated that they never offer coupons for products that they actually use or its never for stables like meat or vegetables and that's not entirely true.

As mentioned earlier, you will want to check coupon sites, newspaper circulars, magazines and the manufacturer website. Also at checkout, the stores usually give you coupons as well.

Following these tips will enable you to get the groceries you get anyway but at lower prices. When you start saving money on discretionary items such as groceries, put the money you saved and put it in your savings account. We will talk about savings in a later chapter.

With car fuel, you will want to utilize apps for your cell phone that help you identify the closest station with the lowest fuel prices and also utilize GPS apps that can help you identify ways to get home faster (time and distance wise) so you can save on fuel costs that you waste getting stuck in stop-and-go traffic. Yes you do waste gas in traffic more than roads and freeways where traffic flows at the same speed longer.

With other discretionary items such as cellphones, you will want to look at your phone patterns and if you have a habit of using less minutes on a regular basis, then maybe its time to lower your phone plan UNLESS you will lose major customer benefits switching plans, then don't do it.

When it comes to spending on eating out or spending on household items, especially if you do it on a regular basis, there are websites where you can get gift cards for major locations at a discount. If you search gift cards at a discount or similar keywords on any major search engine, you will come across websites where you can buy gift cards at a cheaper price. For example, you will have the opportunity to buy let's say a $25.00 gift card for $20 bucks.

Use these gift cards when spending on discretionary items that you buy on a regular basis. You will also want to utilize apps such as iBotta and Shopkick that will give you points or money you can redeem for cash or gift cards just for visiting, checking in and scanning products in places such as department stores, grocery stores, etc.

No matter what you do with any of the aforementioned tips, if you start to save money on a regular basis on things you normally buy such as car fuel, groceries, etc. Always make sure you put the money in your savings or you can do what we will talk about in the next chapter and split 50% into savings and 50% in paying off each debt as you go along.

Chapter 5

Saving Money

The next step in managing your personal finances is to save money. When you start utilizing the tactics in the last chapter you will notice a difference in how much you are spending on things you normally buy every month.

When you start to become creative in how you can buy the things you still want and need for a smaller amount, you will want to put the money you are saving into your bank savings account.

For example, if you normally spend or set a $500 limit on groceries every month and you start utilizing tactics to cut costs and you find out that you now get the same groceries you usually get for $480, then you will put in the $20 you save every month into your savings account. Now, $20 may not seem like much but you will want to have pride that you are able to save any amount of money, even with debt.

Other ways you can utilize to start saving money or obtaining more money to save, is by selling items in your house you no longer need or grew out of.

You can sell these items in a yard sales or sell them online. The point is you will want to sell things you know you no longer will use again, or items you grew out of.

You can also utilize any gift cards people give you especially items that can be used for items you need for your household and purchase with the gift cards instead of cash. The money you save there can also be transferred to your savings account.

If you also notice that you eat out for lunch every day while at work, instead take a lunch to work and save the money you didn't spend by eating out or buy one less coffee every day.

Other tips you can utilize to save money can be:

- Yard sale or sell items you no longer need or want online
- Carpool to work
- Use gift cards you are given to buy household items instead
- Use Coupons and promo codes to cut costs
- Eat out less

- Take up a side job on weekends
- Practice Good driver habits to get discounted insurance rates or a rebate check
- If you have a card with rewards features, use your card to buy household items and then quickly pay the bill
- Use rebate saving apps to redeem points for gift cards
- Contribute to company's 401K to save money without being taxed (keep in mind your after tax income *may be less*).
- Save your pocket change and pick up pennies/change people just lay around
- Buy household items especially if they are on the clearance items at your favorite stores
- Buy generic brands of your favorite items – Trust me, they are the same as the name brands
- Buy in Bulk, you need to calculate this before purchasing but buying in bulk can lead to cost savings.
- Buy gas at stations that are partnered with grocery stores. Usually the grocery stores will give you gas discounts. Sometimes these discounts can be at much as 50cents off per gallon, which will add up over time.

When you start to cut costs, you will notice that the money you will save will add up over time. In time you can take half of what you are saving and use the money to start paying off debts.

In the next chapter, we will cover the proper way to slowly get out of debt.

Chapter 6

Getting Out of Debt

When you start to cut costs, you will start to save a little money that will add up over time. What you can also do as you save money is take half of it and use that for an extra payment for one of your debts.

When you first start this process of improving your personal financial situation, you probably are either late on all of your bills or paying the minimum amounts on your debts. At first, paying the minimum amounts on your bills is a good start because you at least want to pay the minimum amount due and on time.

As you start to save money, you will take half of what you are saving every month and use that to pay off your debts one by one. When choosing which debt to pay off, you will want to choose the debt with the highest monthly payment, but lowest "amount due." This will require either analysis or a careful choice.

I use this formula I learned from other financial experts in the industry. For each debt you have, such as credit cards you want to divide the total amount owed by the minimum monthly payment. You want to do this for all of your debts. For example, let's say you have two credit cards:

Credit Card #1: $5,000 owed with $25 minimum monthly payment.

$$5000/25 = 200$$

Credit Card #2: $10,000 owed with $100 minimum monthly payment

$$10000/100 = 100$$

The numbers 200 and 100 are the minimum number of payments you will need to pay off these debts. This doesn't factor in the interest you are paying every month for not paying the debt off, which is why I said this is the <u>minimum</u> number of payments you will need to make in order to pay off the debt.

In this example, Credit Card #1 will take 200 months minimum to pay off, while Credit Card #2 will only take 100 months. In this case, you will want to use half of the money you are savings every month and either make a higher monthly payment or an extra payment and pay off Credit Card #2 first, even though you owe more.

By using half of the money you are saving every month, and using it to pay off Credit Card #2 faster, once you pay off that debt, you are freeing up another $100 in your monthly budget. What you want to do with that $100 every month and you can either recalculate your budget spreadsheet or keep the old one and just put half of the additional $100 you no longer use to pay off credit card #2 (because its paid off) and put half of it in savings and use the other half and pay your other debts off such as Credit Card #1.

For this strategy to work as fast and as efficiently as possible, you always want to pay off the debt with the lowest # of months after the calculation first! By doing this you will be improving your cash flow over time in the most efficient and quickest manner possible.

The next tip to paying off your debt, is to cut up your credit cards. If you can't use it, then you can't incur any more debt. Keep in mind you want to keep at least one credit card for credit purposes. Even having no credit can hurt you, but we will talk about this more in the next chapter.

Chapter 7

Fixing and Raising Your Credit

The first step in improving your credit is to pay off your debts! The sooner you start to pay off your debts slowly, the sooner your credit score and history will improve.

There are also many tips and tricks you can do to fix your credit and improve your finances:

- Go seek a credit counseling service or consolidation service – be careful of this. Although, you will be saving money by consolidating your payments in one, having this on your credit history can hurt it. Depending on what's important to you, be very careful about making this choice.

- Check your credit – some people are scared to check their credit because it hurts their ego to see the defects in their credit report but you will need to be honest with yourself if you really want to pay off your debt. The other reason why you want to check your credit report and scores from all three of the major bureaus is because you will want to see if all the debts listed there were indeed done by you. In a day and age where fraud is on the rise, it is easy for someone to incur debt under your name. You will want to identify the errors on your report and dispute them, so they can get it taken off your report.

- Inquiries stay on your report for 2 years and debts stay on for a minimum of 7-10 years and bankruptcies stay on for 10 years minimum. You will want to check your credit history to also see if any defects have fallen off your report. If it's past the time required to be on your report, contact the credit bureaus to get it taken off your report. Especially the inquiries, this will help tremendously.

- If you have gotten a control on your bad spending habits, sometimes getting a small store card or credit card and using it wisely and paying it off quickly can also help improve and raise your credit score.

www.ingramcontent.com/pod-product-compliance
Lightning Source LLC
Chambersburg PA
CBHW080532190526
45169CB00008B/3133